21st Century Junior Library

WHAT DOES A SCHOOL BOARD DO?

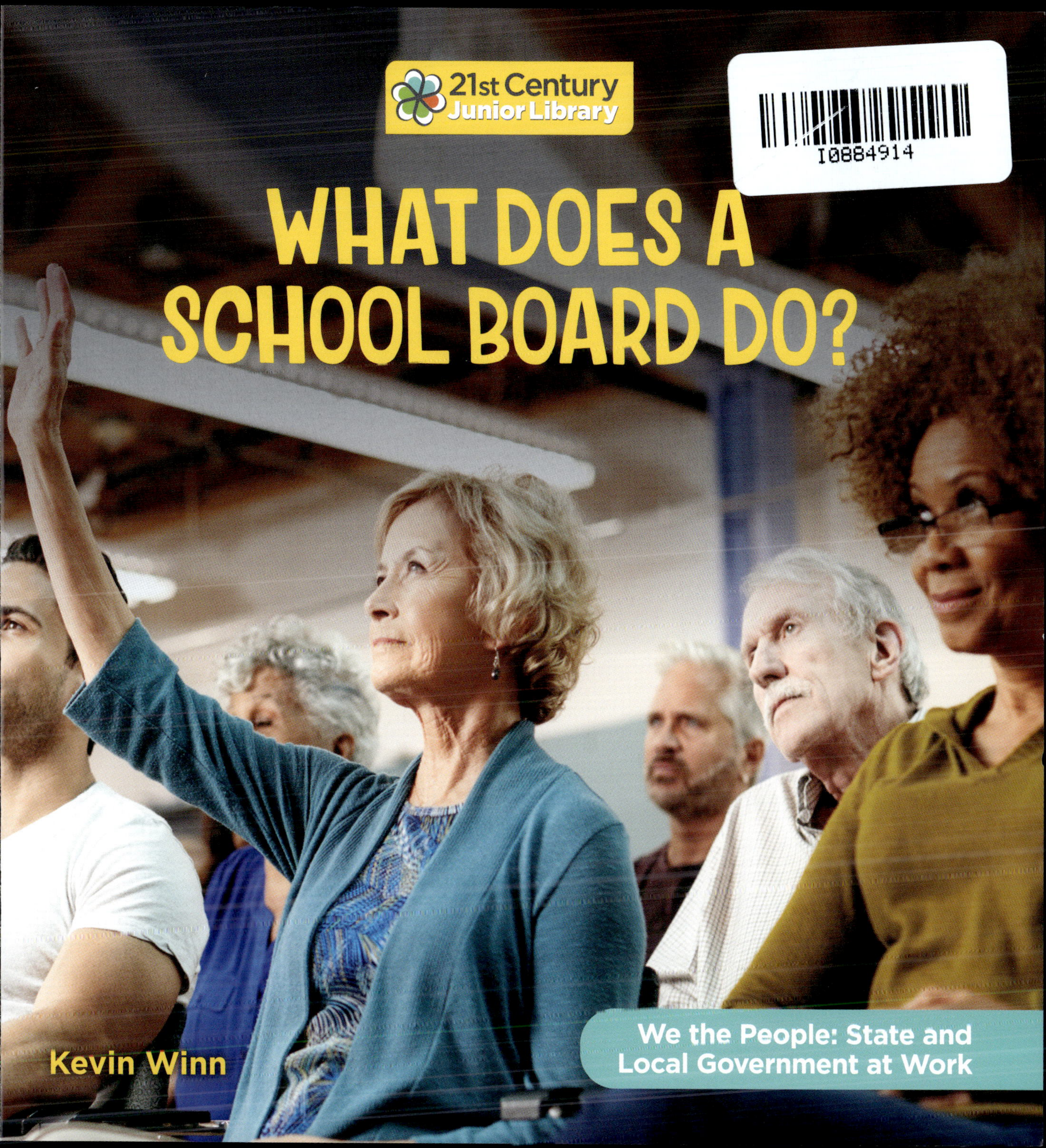

Kevin Winn

We the People: State and Local Government at Work

Published in the United States of America by:

CHERRY LAKE PRESS
2395 South Huron Parkway, Suite 200, Ann Arbor, Michigan 48104
www.cherrylakepress.com

Reading Adviser: Beth Walker Gambro, MS, Ed., Reading Consultant, Yorkville, IL
Content Adviser: Mark Richards, Ph.D., Professor, Dept. of Political Science, Grand Valley State University, Allendale, MI

Photo Credits: © insta_photos/Shutterstock, cover, title page; © digidreamgrafix/Shutterstock, 5; © Gabriele Maltinti/Shutterstock, 6; © New Africa/Shutterstock, 7; © Microgen/Shutterstock, 9; © Dizfoto/Shutterstock, 9; © Prostock-studio/Shutterstock, 10–11; © Elnur/Shutterstock, 13; © DGLimages/Shutterstock, 15; © Morakod1977/Shutterstock, 16; © Matej Kastelic/Shutterstock, 19; © sweet_tomato/Shutterstock, 20; © Drazen Zigic/Shutterstock, 21

Cherry Lake Press is an imprint of Cherry Lake Publishing Group.

Library of Congress Cataloging-in-Publication Data has been filed and is available at catalog.loc.gov.

Cherry Lake Press would like to acknowledge the work of the Partnership for 21st Century Learning, a Network of Battelle for Kids. Please visit Battelle for Kids online for more information.

Printed in the United States of America

CHERRY LAKE PRESS

CONTENTS

Chapter 1: Why Do We Have School Boards? 4

Chapter 2: What Does a School Board Do? 10

Chapter 3: How School Boards Affect Kids 17

Activity 20

Glossary 22

Find Out More 23

Index 24

About the Author 24

WHY DO WE HAVE SCHOOL BOARDS?

All Americans have the right to a free public education. Attending school helps people develop thinking skills and work skills.

As students, you learn different subjects like math, reading, science, and social studies. You might also go to gym class or art class. Your school has many teachers and other people who help the school run smoothly.

Each school is part of a bigger school system.

The school building needs to be taken care of. Some schools have bus systems for students.

Who makes decisions about all these things? For public schools, it's the school board.

Some school districts own their own buses. Some hire bus companies.

A school board is a group of adults who make decisions about how to run schools. Sometimes these adults are elected by voters. Other times, they are **appointed** by the city mayor or another elected official.

Every state has school districts. Most towns have their own district. In many school districts, people **campaign** for a position on the school board. They ask people to vote for them. Like people who run for mayor, president, or state legislator, they share their ideas. They ask voters to trust that they will make good decisions about public education.

Ask Questions!

School board members make many decisions about how to spend money. They must decide what will help the district most. What are some questions you have about how the school board spends money in your district?

In other school districts, the school board members are appointed by the mayor or another elected official.

States have school boards, too. State school boards make decisions for the whole state. State school boards may be elected or appointed by the governor. States run their own schools. But they have to follow federal laws like civil rights laws.

State school boards decide what students in that state should learn.

WHAT DOES A SCHOOL BOARD DO?

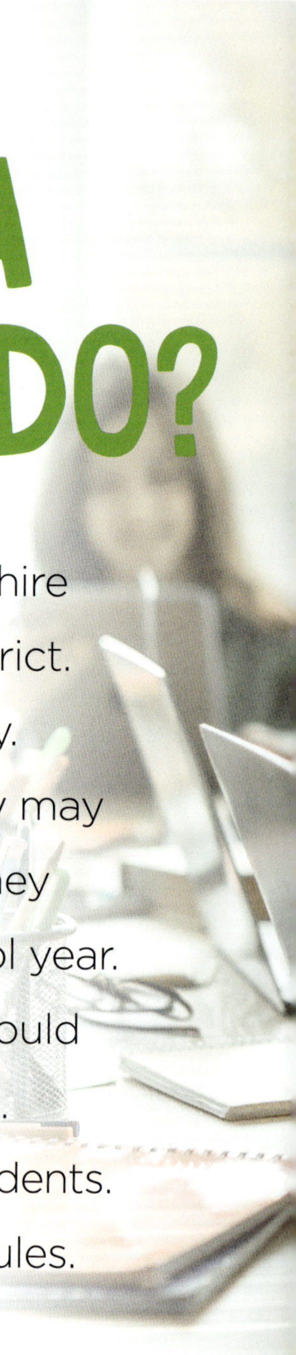

School boards have important duties. They hire the **superintendent**, who leads the school district. They decide how to spend the district's money. They write **policies**, or rules. For example, they may decide if there will be a student dress code. They set the length of the school day and the school year.

The school board decides what students should learn. They think about the kids in their district. They want to meet the learning needs of all students. However, the school board must follow state rules.

Certain school decisions are made at the state level. For example, state officials create **standards**, or guidelines, about what kids learn in their classes.

The school board makes sure the superintendent is doing his or her job well. They also meet with parents and other community members. This helps families have a say in their children's education. Parents and community members can also bring questions and complaints to the school board.

Create!

School boards help write new district rules or change existing ones. What is one rule your school or district has that you would like to change? Write a letter to your school board explaining why. Support your argument with at least two reasons.

The school board must make sure that all students have what they need for a good education. This is a huge job. Students have different needs and learn in different ways.

In many districts, school board members are elected from different neighborhoods. This helps make sure that all neighborhoods in the district have someone to speak for them.

Some districts have at-large school board members. An at-large member can come from any neighborhood. This may mean one neighborhood has more representatives than the others.

Make a Guess!

Every school has needs. Teachers need to be paid. Students need resources like science equipment and library books. But a school board does not have unlimited money. What might happen if the school board runs out of money? Who would be affected?

School boards spend a lot of time talking about money. They decide what to do with the money they receive from taxes and other sources. They form a **budget** to decide how much money to spend on different programs. They might decide how much teachers are paid or how much to spend on books or equipment.

School boards work to help schools meet student needs.

Look!

School boards meet often. Students can attend these meetings. Watch one of these meetings online or in person. Take notes on what school board members discuss. Write down three things that surprise you.

HOW SCHOOL BOARDS AFFECT KIDS

The school board makes decisions about ideas that affect students every day. They work with the superintendent on these decisions. As a team, they might work to set the school calendar. They may also decide how much money to spend on new playgrounds, choose student textbooks, or build new schools.

Most school boards have only adult members. But some school districts want to hear directly from students. In these districts, student representatives serve on the school board. These representatives give their opinions on decisions that affect them and their fellow students.

School board meetings are public. Anyone can attend and take part in the discussion. If you sign up before the meeting, you can ask to speak about a topic that's important to you. Sometimes many people line up to speak at school board meetings. People have a lot to say about education!

Think!

Kids who run for school board must get elected. If you wanted to be the student representative on the school board, how would you convince your classmates to vote for you? Write a paragraph that includes three reasons why you are the best person for the job.

ACTIVITY

WRITE IT OUT! What is a part of life at school that you care about? What might you like to say to the school board on this topic? Write a paragraph to share with your school board.

GLOSSARY

appointed (uh-POYNT-uhd) selected to fill an office or job

budget (BUH-jut) a spending plan

campaign (kam-PAYN) to run for an elected position

policies (PAH-luh-seez) official rules

standards (STAN-durdz) in education, a list of learning goals for students at each grade level

superintendent (soo-pur-in-TEN-duhnt) a leader of the school district

FIND OUT MORE

Books

Bedesky, Baron. *What is a Government?* New York, NY: Crabtree Publishing Co., 2008.

Christelow, Eileen. *Vote!* New York, NY: Clarion Books, 2018.

Let's Go Local!: Role of Branches in Local Government in the US. Baby Professor, 2022.

Websites

Search these online sources with an adult.

Local Government for Kids | Miacademy Learning Channel | YouTube
Learn how local government works.

iCivics
Find out how you can be an informed and involved citizen.

INDEX

activities, 20
appointments, 7, 9
at-large board members, 15

budgeting, 8, 14, 15, 17
bus transportation, 6

curriculum standards, 10, 12

decision making, 6–7, 8, 10, 12, 14, 15, 17

educational standards, 10, 12
elections, 7, 8, 19

learning, 4, 10, 12

meetings, 16, 18

policies and rules, 10, 12
political appointments, 7, 9
public education, 4

roles and responsibilities, 6–7, 10–15, 17

school boards
  communication, 8, 16, 18, 20
  meetings, 16, 18
  members, 7, 14–15, 18
  roles and responsibilities, 6–7, 10–15, 17
  state-level, 9
spending decisions, 8, 14, 15, 17
state school boards, 9
state standards, 10, 12
student needs, 10–12, 14, 18, 19, 20
superintendents, 10, 12, 17

ABOUT THE AUTHOR

Kevin Winn is a children's book writer and researcher. He focuses on issues of racial justice and educational equity in his work. In 2020, Kevin earned his doctorate in Educational Policy and Evaluation from Arizona State University.